ALEX MCCORMICK

The 21 Day Prayer Playbook

Discover How Jesus Prayed To Win!

Copyright © 2025 by Alex McCormick

All rights reserved. No part of this publication may be reproduced, stored or transmitted in any form or by any means, electronic, mechanical, photocopying, recording, scanning, or otherwise without written permission from the publisher. It is illegal to copy this book, post it to a website, or distribute it by any other means without permission.

Alex McCormick asserts the moral right to be identified as the author of this work.

Alex McCormick has no responsibility for the persistence or accuracy of URLs for external or third-party Internet Websites referred to in this publication and does not guarantee that any content on such Websites is, or will remain, accurate or appropriate.

Designations used by companies to distinguish their products are often claimed as trademarks. All brand names and product names used in this book and on its cover are trade names, service marks, trademarks and registered trademarks of their respective owners. The publishers and the book are not associated with any product or vendor mentioned in this book. None of the companies referenced within the book have endorsed the book.

First edition

This book was professionally typeset on Reedsy. Find out more at reedsy.com

First to my God. This was Your idea. Thank You for speaking this short work into my heart. To my wife Colleen and my children. You guys are my greatest gift from God. To my church family, I love you all. To my Pastor Dr. Edward Ramirez, your example has changed my life and I love and honor you and Mel. Finally to the men who mentored and spoke into my life and have since graduated, Pastor David Demola, Dr. Myles Munroe and Pastor Bob Evans, I honor you. I dedicate this book to all of you!

"The evidence of your desire is in your pursuit son…"

DR. EDWARD RAMIREZ

Contents

Introduction		ii
1	What is Prayer?	1
2	How Jesus Taught Us to Pray - Lordship	5
3	How Jesus Taught Us to Pray - Intercession	19
4	How Jesus Taught Us to Pray - Petition	24
5	7 Prayers of Lordship	32
6	7 Prayers of Intercession	42
7	7 Prayers of Petition	52
8	Conclusion	62

Introduction

Imagine with me for a moment that you and I are walking on the earth at the same time Jesus is alive. You and I will be the second string disciples. Now all this time we've been with Jesus and seeing the blind receive their sight, the cripple walk, and people whose skin is literally melting off of them all of a sudden get new skin. Are you with me so far? Everywhere we go we are seeing miracle after miracle happen in the lives of everyone Jesus touches. Then one day as we're waking up to start another day unsure of what it will bring one of us musters the strength to ask Jesus a question… If that were you, what would that question be?

If it were me I might ask Jesus where he was hiding all those fish and bread we fed the 5000 men the other day. Or I might wonder, how did you wake that dead girl during her own funeral last month? Fortunately for you, I wasn't there this particular day, but one of the disciples had the wisdom to ask the question that would take center stage in the lives of every Christ follower since then. Luke 11:1 the disciple asks, "… **Lord, teach us how to pray…**"

Now something that should be clearly understood here is that the disciples knew what prayer was. They were Jewish boys and even if their families were not devout, they had a picture of prayer around them constantly. In fact when this disciple asked Jesus to teach them, he referenced John the Baptist basically asking Jesus to teach them like John taught his disciples. I sometimes wonder, why ask at this point for Jesus to teach them prayer. Jesus was obviously winning in every area of his life and I believe that was the point. With all of the Rabbis of the day around, and the nature of the Jewish lifestyle where the synagogue was at the center of everything in their culture, they knew very well what prayer was. However, Jesus was praying and getting different results than the Rabbis.

This book is designed to help you understand how Jesus taught us to pray and get results. One of the challenges I've seen over the last 25 years of ministry is that people will pray but if they don't get the result they want, they think prayer doesn't work and stop praying. **PRAYER WORKS** if you know how to work it. So let's get ready to exercise our faith and learn from Jesus himself how to pray..

In Luke chapter eleven and eighteen, Jesus taught three primary ways to pray: first the prayer of Lordship(11:1-4), The prayer of Intercession(11:5-8), and The prayer of Petition(18:1-8). The first half of this book is dedicated to bringing understanding to these prayers. The second half of this book I will outline for you 21 prayer points to consider when praying over the course of 21 days. To be clear, this is not a comprehensive prayer guide, in fact we will just really scratch the surface in this book. I could write a textbook drilling down into the nitty gritty of these prayers and give you more than a hundred prayer points. The purpose of this short book is to give you principles of prayer that will change the way you pray and see results in your life. If you are a new Christ-follower, I'm especially rooting for you to get through this book and start a life of prayer that gets results. If you've been following Christ for a long time… Read this book! It will encourage you to keep on praying.

1

What is Prayer?

Defining prayer should be relatively simple. To sum up what most people think prayer is in simple terms, it is communication to God. To be clear I don't disagree with this definition, but I believe that in order to really comprehend the power of prayer for us, we must understand the full context of what God expects of us when we pray. Consider these two scriptures:

*"For unto us a Child is born, Unto us a Son is given; And **the government will be upon His shoulder**. And His name will be called Wonderful, Counselor, Mighty God, Everlasting Father, Prince of Peace. **Of the increase of His government and peace There will be no end...**" Isaiah 9:6-7a NKJV*

*"From that time Jesus began to preach and to say, "Repent, **for the kingdom of heaven is at hand**." Matthew 4:17 NKJV*

These two and many more scriptures reference the very nature of what Jesus came to re-establish when he came to earth. Isaiah said that he would have a government on His shoulders and that government would continue to increase forever. Once Jesus physically shows up to the earth, and grows into fulfilling his calling, he goes into the wilderness and fasts for forty days and nights. After returning and being tempted by Satan, he preaches a one point sermon and that is to repent (change the way you think) because the Kingdom is here within reach.

The reason I emphasize this point is so you understand from the very beginning that prayer is not a religious act. Jesus did not come to earth to re-establish a religion, he came to re-establish the Kingdom of Heaven. What we lost from the beginning was not a religion, what we lost was the reign of the King in our hearts.

Now in a Kingdom the most important person is the King and in any form of government there are laws, a constitution, and governing structures. The most important thing to understand about the Kingdom for most people that will read this book is that a Kingdom is not a democracy. We don't vote on things in the Kingdom because law is established by the word of the King. The other important principle of Kingdom to know is that every citizen of a Kingdom is a representation of that King. For that reason it is in the King's best interest to ensure that His people are well taken care of, especially if that King plans to enlarge His territory.

So now in the context of the Kingdom, what is prayer? Simply put, prayer is a petition. If you know anything about law, a petition is a legal way of accessing the rights that you have as a citizen of any government. If ever you are in a legal dispute and your rights have been violated you go to court and petition the judge to rule according to the law and re-establish your rights as a citizen. The best part is that the judge represents the government, so when a ruling comes in your favor, the full weight of the government is behind that ruling and must work for you.

Before we dive into the different types of prayer Jesus prayed, consider this scripture:

*"This is the confidence which we have before Him, that, if we ask anything **according to His will**, He hears us. And if we know that He hears us in whatever we ask, **we know that we have the requests which we have asked from Him**." 1 John 5:14-15 NKJV*

This scripture is a reminder to me that when I bring my petition to the Lord, there has to be legal precedent for my request. The scripture tells us that our petition is granted when we ask according to His will. Remember, God's word is full of precedent to see that we His citizens are well taken care of, so we need to know what God's word says about us. The flip side of that principle is to also remember that God cannot answer a petition that goes against His word.

As we begin to examine the types of prayer Jesus taught us to pray, examine your prayer life and ensure that you are praying according to the Word of God. If you've been wrong and not praying in faith, **CHANGE THE WAY YOU PRAY**! If you stopped praying a long time ago thinking, "Prayer doesn't really work." I'd like to encourage you to begin this journey of faith with me again through this book and by faith in the Word of

God shared here. Lastly, if what I've said so far resonates with you, be sure to get a book for a brother or sister in Christ that you know needs to rekindle the fire for prayer, and go through this together and encourage each other in the Lord!

Receive this prayer for you:

Lord, I thank you for the people that you have led to this book to grow in knowing You, fanning the fire for prayer in their own lives. Thank You for revealing Yourself to each one in a special way and anointing their eyes and ears to receive Your Word, in Jesus name... Amen!

2

How Jesus Taught Us to Pray - Lordship

"Now it came to pass, as He was praying in a certain place, when He ceased, that one of His disciples said to Him, "Lord, teach us to pray, as John also taught his disciples." So He said to them, "When you pray, say: Our Father in heaven, Hallowed be Your name. Your kingdom come. Your will be done On earth as it is in heaven. Give us day by day our daily bread. And forgive us our sins, For we also forgive everyone who is indebted to us. And do not lead us into temptation, But deliver us from the evil one." - Luke 11:1-4

Here in Luke chapter 11 we see the first of three main texts that we will examine to understand the mind of King Jesus when we pray. The first thing I'll point out about this and the other prayers is that Jesus is giving us a model for prayer. The words in and of themselves are inconsequential without offering this prayer in faith from your heart. Prayer is not an experiment you try to see if it works or not... **PRAYER WORKS**, when you know how to work it! So to be clear before you come to the Lord to ask for anything - as my dad used to say - do a heart check! Consider what God's Word says about your heart:

*"As in water a face reflects the face, **so the heart of a person reflects the person.**" - Proverbs 27:19 NASB*

*"But the LORD said to Samuel, "Do not look at his appearance or at his physical stature, because I have refused him. For the LORD does not see as man sees; for man looks at the outward appearance, **but***

the Lord looks at the heart." - *1 Samuel 16:7 NKJV*

"Our Father…"

As we reflect on the prayer Jesus is teaching the disciples here in Luke 11, he first starts with, "Our Father…" which in ancient Hebrew is the word transliterated, "Abba." Now some more scholarly will point out that the New Testament was written in Greek which I agree with but Jesus wasn't speaking Greek to these Hebrew boys and it's important for us to understand the significance of the father in Jewish culture. In ancient Hebrew and Aramaic, names weren't just names like they are today. Father wasn't just a title in their culture, Father was a function. So when they prayed, "Our Father," Jesus was encouraging them to recognize God as their source. In their culture the Rabbis were their intermediary, but Jesus removed the intermediary and connected them directly to the source.

This is so important for us to understand! Jesus came and died to restore the Kingdom to the earth and that also meant re-establishing the direct connection we have with God. That is what Adam had in the garden and that is what we lost because of sin. So be grateful even more today for the restoration of the relationship you have with the Father and when you call on Him, know that His name is what He is, the primary source of our lives!

"In heaven"

Next Jesus prays, "in heaven." Heaven is simply a place, and in the context of the Kingdom, think of heaven as another country. Heaven is the country or territory where the King completely dominates and rules. We read about this place all throughout scripture and will talk about it more in the next couple of chapters.

"Hallowed be Your name"

The word hallowed can also be replaced with the word holy. It simply means to be set apart for special use. Remember that names in the Hebrew culture were given to capture the function of the person. While I will not do a deep dive into the names of God in this book, I will say that God gave us his name to reveal Himself and His nature to us. So when Jesus says hallowed or holy, it is an act of worship and again recognizing who God is.

This is super important and worth at least dipping our feet in here. Did you know that our primary role as citizen sons and daughters in the Kingdom is to worship God? To be clear I'm not talking about singing and playing music. Those are great expressions and extensions of worship, but music is not worship unless it is coming from a worshipper. Worship is a lifestyle! My primary prayer is, "God let my life be a worship song to you." That means that in everything I do I'm glorifying God. In every interaction I'm filtering my thoughts and actions through the filter of my love relationship with God. Sure there are times I fail, my attitude isn't great, I'm being selfish, impatient, or any number of other things. I fail sometimes because I have to deal with my flesh which literally wants to drag me the opposite direction of where God is leading me. I thank God that He never leaves because when I find myself off track, He makes getting back on track simple. Consider what the scripture says:

*"If we say that we have no sin, we deceive ourselves, and the truth is not in us. **If we confess our sins, He is faithful and just to forgive us our sins and to cleanse us from all unrighteousness.**"*
- 1 John 1:8-9 NKJV

To stay right in our worship life, we must live lives of repentance. It is not ok to knowingly sin and just keep on going like nothing happened. You must confess your sin to God. Did you notice the scripture doesn't say we have to beg for forgiveness, or feel bad for the rest of your life about what you did. No! Tell God you're wrong, turn your back to the sin and continue to pursue the things of the Kingdom! As worshipers of God we find our worth in God who is the object of our worship, so worship His name and prioritize His Kingdom in your life!

"Your Kingdom come. Your will be done."

Here I believe is the primary petition of this prayer. After we have recognized God as Father and worshiped His name, we ask that, "Your Kingdom come. Your will be done." To understand the weight of this prayer you have to understand how a kingdom works. If you split the word up you have two parts, "King," and "domain." Simply put a kingdom is a place where the king has complete authority and the will of the king is law. So this is now the most transformational prayer you will ever pray, because when we say to God, "Let Your kingdom come and Your will be done," we are now surrendering our right to rule our own lives. Think about the depth of that for a moment... you are trading your way of thinking and doing what you have always done to surrender complete control to God.

The reason this point is so important to understand is because many Christians come to Jesus confessing Him as Lord of their lives, and settle for just going to heaven one day. Nothing really changes... you think the same way and you do the same things you've always done, except now you go to church on Sundays. At some point you get frustrated thinking, "Well I'm going to church, why aren't things getting better?" Let me say that going to church is a super important part of your walk, but what without surrendering your world to God, all you're doing is living a double life and you can only do that for so long before you either go one way or the other. Consider what Jesus said about your priorities as a citizen son or daughter:

"Therefore do not worry, saying, 'What shall we eat?' or 'What shall we drink?' or 'What shall we wear?' For after all these things the Gentiles seek. For your heavenly Father knows that you need all these things. **But seek first the kingdom of God and His righteousness, and all these things shall be added to you.**" - Matthew 6:31-33

Jesus is literally telling us to let the King rule our lives and the things we have been so concerned about getting will be added to us automatically. Let me help you understand this in question form. Take a moment and think about the things that concern you the most right now. **Now if you were living in heaven would those things still concern you?** You see the power in this part of the prayer is that you are literally calling on the Kingdom to come. Think about that.. You don't have to die to experience heaven because Jesus is literally teaching you how to pray heaven to earth.

When you understand this the miracles, signs, and wonders that were always happening around Jesus make more sense. There is no sickness in heaven so if Jesus brought heaven to earth, naturally anyone who was around him would experience heaven as well. So the blind eyes opened, crippled people danced in the street and funeral processions became a lot of fun! This revelation has changed the way I pray in this regard, because I really don't need to pray for 'things' as much, if I petition the Kingdom to come to my life.

So I gladly give up my rights to truly make Jesus the Lord of my life. I will accomplish more and worry less when I hand over the reins of my life. I will not be worried about whether I am doing what I'm supposed to be doing when I give Him Lordship in my life. The Word of God tells me in no uncertain terms that the steps of the righteous are ordered by the Lord. If He is Lord over every step, there is no need for anxiety or impatience. There is no cause for stress, fear, or confusion. If I were you, I'd petition for the Lordship of the King everyday! My personal petition of the Lord regularly is, "Lord, let your Kingdom come and let Your will be done in me. Whatever You choose to do, Lord do it in me!" Come on... If you want that

Lordship in your life, petition the King right now:

"Lord, let your Kingdom come and let Your will be done in me. Whatever You choose to do, Lord do it in me!"

"On earth as it is in heaven."

Remember earlier when I said to think of heaven as a country? Just like any country the Kingdom has the characteristics of a country. There is a culture in the Kingdom that is shaped by God's Word. What Jesus is petitioning for is the culture of the Kingdom to expand into our lives here on earth. To help you understand this a little better, I'd compare this expansion to what we refer to as colonization. In basic terms colonization is when a Kingdom takes its culture and expands it to a new territory. For example, Centuries ago there were and still are some places that are ruled by a monarchy. Spain, France, and England are the three that stand out to me the most. A King's goal is always to expand his territory, so if you travel to different islands in the Caribbean you will find when visiting the Bahamas, they still have high tea and speak English because long ago they were colonized by England. However, if you go to Guyana you may hear French being spoken or Spanish in Cuba.

The point here is that when Jesus prays, "on earth as it is in heaven." It's not just an angel or something mystical that comes, but the whole culture of heaven comes. Yes, that comes with the language of faith, and a higher sense of morality. When the Kingdom comes to earth our responsibility is to immerse ourselves in that culture of the King with the help of the Holy Spirit until we become a true representation of the Kingdom of God on the earth.

"Give us day by day our daily bread"

One of the parts of God's character that we see early on in scripture is that He is interested in everyday being fresh and new. In the book of Exodus God answers the complaining of the children of Israel with a supply of bread and meat everyday except the sabbath. God told the children of Israel to take what they need for the day, and He would supply them fresh bread and meat everyday in the wilderness. Of course, Israel was not fully compliant and some tried to keep a supply for the next day to find the leftovers spoiled and moldy the next morning.

God wants us to experience His fresh word, fresh anointing, and fresh outpouring of his goodness and mercy everyday. All over the Bible you will find God giving us promises of new, fresh, everyday blessings. Consider these scriptures::

"Through the LORD's mercies we are not consumed, because His compassions fail not. ***They are new every morning****; Great is Your faithfulness." - Lamentations 3:22-23 NKJV*

"Surely goodness and mercy shall follow me ***all the days of my life****; And I will [d]dwell in the house of the LORD Forever." - Psalm 23:6 NKJV*

*"Blessed be the Lord, **Who daily loads us with benefits**, The God of our salvation! Selah"* - *Psalm 68:19 NKJV*

As a father and a husband, I love to prepare and enjoy a fresh meal with my family. That is something I would love to do everyday, and although I personally cannot do that in this season, God doesn't batch cook to keep His kids fed for days. His word is fresh everyday, so when Jesus teaches us to pray this way, we have to see God as the one who truly sustains us. I believe God's desire is to have a people sustained by His word. He will re-fire and restore you if you need it, but could you imagine a life where your fire for God burned constantly without even looking like it's going out. Let's look to Him and His Word everyday to sustain us!

"And forgive us our sins, For we also forgive everyone who is indebted to us."

One of the hardest steps we will ever have to take in our lives is to forgive people who really owe us something. It could be an apology for some wrong done to you, or someone breaking their word and not doing what they said they would do. It could be an actual debt like money or services, or even something more serious that brought you physical and mental harm. Whatever the situation, we have to understand that unforgiveness in our lives will hinder answered prayer.

I've had the privilege of walking with a lot of my brothers and sister through this process of forgiveness and have had to walk through it for myself. I know the first thing that we could say to God is, "But, you don't know what he or she did to me…" I have been in this place and first let me help understand that God knows exactly what was done. Consider this scripture:

*"Remember the former things of old, For I am God, and there is no other; I am God, and there is none like Me, **declaring the end from the beginning, and from ancient times things that are not yet done...**"* - Isaiah 46:9-10a

God knows everything that others have done and yet He gives us the super power to forgive anyway. He knows something about being hurt and then forgiving anyway. We can look time after time as the children of Israel complained after being set free from the Egyptians. How they erected and worshiped a golden calf while Moses was away. How they wandered in the wilderness for forty years because of a generation of unbelieving Jews who wouldn't take God at his word. When we forward wind to the time Jesus lived, religious Jews crucified Jesus. Was Jesus' death part of the plan of our redemption? Yes! But it took bitter and religious people who should have known who Jesus truly was to crucify him. Look what Paul said about his death to the Romans:

*"But God demonstrates His own love toward us, in that **while we were still sinners, Christ died for us.**"* - Romans 5:8 NKJV

So when Jesus instructs us to pray for our forgiveness, it is not by mistake that He attaches our ability to forgive others to this prayer. This principle of forgiveness extends beyond just answered prayer. Look what Matthew records Jesus saying:

*"Therefore if you bring your gift to the altar, and there remember that your brother has something against you, leave your gift there before the altar, and go your way. **First be reconciled to your brother**, and then come and offer your gift." - Matthew 5:23-24 NKJV*

So again this goes back to your heart. It's time for a heart check. If you have anything against your brother, sister, friend, enemy, or anyone in between, forgiveness is your next step in receiving all that God has for you.

"And do not lead us into temptation, But deliver us from the evil one."

At the first reading of this portion of the prayer I used to think that I had to ask God not to lead me the wrong way. To bring clarity to this portion of the prayer, consider what James says on this subject:

*"Blessed is the man who endures temptation; for when he has been approved, he will receive the crown of life which the Lord has promised to those who love Him. **Let no one say when he is tempted, 'I am tempted by God'**; for God cannot be tempted by evil, **nor does He Himself tempt anyone.**" - James 1:12-13 NKJV*

So if God doesn't tempt anyone, what is Jesus actually praying here? To put it simply this prayer could also read, **"Help us to follow Your Spirit and discern when we are pushing the boundaries of Your will for our lives."** In other words Lord help me not to step out of bounds. When we read further in

James, he actually gives more explanation for where temptation in our lives comes from:

*"But each one is tempted when **he is drawn away by his own desires** and enticed. Then, when desire has conceived, it gives birth to sin; and sin, when it is full-grown, brings forth death." - James 1:14-15 NKJV*

This is where we circle back to understanding the culture of the Kingdom of God. When we are in sin without the Kingdom ruling in our hearts, our desires are naturally going to feed our flesh. In other words, our flesh desires what looks good, feels good, smells good, tastes good, and sounds good. When we are led by our flesh, our desires are all sensually driven. I am not old, but I have learned in my short time here on earth that just looking, feeling, smelling, tasting, or sounding good doesn't make it good for you. However, being born in sin and growing up catering to our sensuality makes it very challenging to ignore your flesh. In his letter to the Romans Paul gives us this prescription for this issue:

*"Therefore, brethren, we are debtors—not to the flesh, to live according to the flesh. For if you live according to the flesh you will die; **but if by the Spirit you put to death the deeds of the body, you will live.**" Romans 8:12-13 NKJV*

So when we pray this last part of the prayer, it is a cry to God to again establish His Kingdom in us so that our Spirit man, made in his image, takes control. When that happens our desires will change, and our focus will be to do what God wants for our lives, instead of just avoiding sin. Don't waste energy trying to avoid sinning! Get the Word of God in you and pursue the Kingdom with your life and you will naturally avoid sin and any traps of Satan.

My pastor, Dr. Edward Ramirez, said to me one time, "The evidence of your desire is in your pursuit son!" Since the first time I heard him say that more than ten years ago that has stuck with me. If your desire is for the benefits of the Kingdom of God, you will adjust your pursuit to match your desire. Where many times the enemy traps us is in thinking that we can continue to feed our flesh whatever it wants and still have all of God. This is just not true. Please don't get me wrong, if you're reading this and your life is jacked up, know that God loves you. However, love will never leave you in the ditch it found you. So it may not feel real good to your flesh, but this is a call for you to put your prayer and fasting life at the top of your list of priorities and pursue God with all your heart!

3

How Jesus Taught Us to Pray - Intercession

> "And He said to them, "Which of you shall have a friend, and go to him at midnight and say to him, 'Friend, lend me three loaves; for a friend of mine has come to me on his journey, and I have nothing to set before him'; and he will answer from within and say, 'Do not trouble me; the door is now shut, and my children are with me in bed; I cannot rise and give to you'? I say to you, though he will not rise and give to him because he is his friend, yet because of his persistence he will rise and give him as many as he needs." - Luke 11:5-8 NKJV

The second form of prayer Jesus prays is immediately following the prayer of Lordship in Luke 11. This is the prayer of Intercession. To be an intercessor is simply to be a bridge between God and another person in your life. Intercession is not a prayer that you pray for yourself, but it is you standing in the gap for someone else that has a need.

Notice in this teaching on intercession Jesus refers to the three people involved in this prayer. There is the friend in need, the neighbor with a full supply, and an intercessor who stands in the middle with relationships to both of these individuals. I think it's interesting that when the intercessor goes to the neighbor, the scripture tells us it's at midnight. Many times when we see things happening at midnight in the Bible, it signifies the worst possible time in someone's life, and sometimes the time that God begins to move on their behalf:

"Who, having received such a charge, thrust them into the inner

prison, and made their feet fast in the stocks. And **at midnight Paul and Silas prayed, and sang praises unto God: and the prisoners heard them.** *And suddenly there was a great earthquake, so that* **the foundations of the prison were shaken:** *and immediately all the doors were opened, and every one's bands were loosed." -* Acts 16:24-26 NKJV

"The bands of the wicked have robbed me: but I have not forgotten thy law. **At midnight I will rise to give thanks unto thee because of thy righteous judgments."** *-* Psalm 119:61-62 NKJV

"For his anger endureth but a moment; in his favour is life: **weeping may endure for a night, but joy cometh in the morning."** *-* Psalm 30:5 NKJV

The other extremely important thing to note here is that the intercessor recognized that he did not have what was needed for the friend in need. There are often times when someone comes to me for counsel and I don't have the answer. So my position now becomes that of an intercessor to say to the Holy Spirit, "I don't have the wisdom to navigate my brother through this situation… Would You give me supernatural wisdom to help?" I have to tell you that leaning into the Holy Spirit for answers is the most liberating thing in the world. I can literally look a person in the eye and say, "I don't know, but let me knock on the Holy Spirit's door, because I may not have what you need, but I know who does!

Let me also add a disclaimer and a warning about intercession. First, there is no office of intercessor in the scripture, nor is there a gift of intercession. That means we can all intercede as long as we have access to the King. He is the One with the supply, so let's not even think or attempt to take credit or glory for something that God has done. I want to personally thank you right now for standing in the gap on behalf of others, but God will not share His glory with anyone as evidenced by the anointed cherub that was cast out of heaven like lightning.

Secondly, the need of the friend that you are interceding for should not be burdensome for you. I have seen so many people over the years fall into depression over things or people they are supposed to be standing in the gap and praying for. The burden does not belong to you, it belongs to God. He can handle it and we can not. Consider what Peter says:

"Therefore humble yourselves under the mighty hand of God [set aside self-righteous pride], so that He may exalt you [to a place of honor in His service] at the appropriate time, **casting all your cares [all your anxieties, all your worries, and all your concerns, once and for all] on Him, for He cares about you [with deepest affection, and watches over you very carefully]. Be sober [well balanced and self-disciplined], be alert and cautious at all times.** *That enemy of yours, the devil, prowls around like a roaring lion [fiercely hungry], seeking someone to devour." - 1 Peter 5:6-8 AMP*

Consider intercession as a trusted position God has put you in, so that he can reach through you to answer that prayer.

The last part of what Jesus teaches us about intercession is persistence in prayer. Notice the bread was not given just because of the relationship, it was given because of persistence.

Consider what Luke writes immediately following this passage:

"So I say to you, ask and keep on asking, and it will be given to you; seek and keep on seeking, and you will find; knock and keep on knocking, and the door will be opened to you. **For everyone who keeps on asking [persistently], receives; and he who keeps on seeking [persistently], finds; and to him who keeps on knocking [persistently], the door will be opened."** - Luke 11:9-10 AMP

Sometimes I have prayed for things and had immediate peace about it, but sometimes I felt the need to pray with more persistence. Interestingly enough I remember being taught growing up that you just pray once in faith and praise God for the results. I actually think there is merit to that, but I would also add that praying persistently is not praying until you have faith. It is praying in faith consistently that yields the results that you prayed for. So persistence in intercession is key!

4

How Jesus Taught Us to Pray - Petition

> "Then He spoke a parable to them, that men always ought to pray and not lose heart, saying: "There was in a certain city a judge who did not fear God nor regard man. Now there was a widow in that city; and she came to him, saying, 'Get justice for me from my adversary.' And he would not for a while; but afterward he said within himself, 'Though I do not fear God nor regard man, yet because this widow troubles me I will avenge her, lest by her continual coming she weary me.' " Then the Lord said, "Hear what the unjust judge said. And shall God not avenge His own elect who cry out day and night to Him, though He bears long with them? I tell you that He will avenge them speedily. Nevertheless, when the Son of Man comes, will He really find faith on the earth?" - Luke 18:1-8 NKJV

I love the way Jesus introduces this third type of prayer, "...men always ought to pray **and not lose heart**..." I think our view of prayer can be microwave driven in thought sometimes. We are looking many times for things to move swiftly, and there's no doubt that God does do things swiftly and in the moment a prayer is offered. However, It is important to understand that not every prayer we pray will yield a sensational result in the moment. There are some areas of our lives that we will need to pray in faith continually to see what God will do.

I can hear some hearts saying, "How long do I have to pray?" To answer that I skip to the end of the prayer and ask are you willing to stand in faith no matter what it looks like now? At the end of the day God is still looking for faith to receive what He will do in your life.

In the book of Daniel chapters nine and ten, Daniel has two very different experiences in prayer that I would like you to consider as you take the time to petition God. In chapter nine Daniel is praying and repenting for the sins of the people of Israel and verse twenty reveals something very interesting:

*"**While I was still speaking and praying**, and confessing my sin and the sin of my people Israel, and presenting my supplication before the LORD my God in behalf of the holy mountain of my God, **while I was still speaking in prayer** and extremely exhausted, the man Gabriel, whom I had seen in the earlier vision, came to me about the time of the evening sacrifice. He instructed me and he talked with me and said, "O Daniel, **I have now come to give you insight and wisdom and understanding**." - Daniel 9:20-22 AMP*

Notice in this passage Daniel wasn't even done praying and Gabriel was already there with an answer to his prayer. Now this wasn't a short 30 second prayer if he was exhausted, but I love the fact that God shows up in the middle of this prayer, because it shows me that God nature is to answer the prayers of His people. Jeremiah prophecy's it this way:

*"Then you will call on Me and you will come and pray to Me, and **I will hear [your voice] and I will listen to you**." - Jeremiah 29:12 AMP*

I love it when answers come sooner than later, and they have for me many times, but after Daniel gets his answer in chapter nine, just a chapter later look at the timing of God's answer:

*"In those days **I, Daniel, had been mourning for three entire weeks**... Then I heard the sound of his words; and when I heard the sound of his words, I fell on my face in a deep sleep, with my face toward the ground. Then behold, a hand touched me and set me unsteadily on my hands and knees. So he said to me, "O Daniel, you highly regarded and greatly beloved man, understand the words that I am about to say to you and stand upright, for I have now been sent to you." And while he was saying this word to me, I stood up trembling. Then he said to me, "Do not be afraid, Daniel, for **from the first day that you set your heart on understanding this and on humbling yourself before your God, your words were heard**, and I have come in response to your words." Daniel 10:2, 9-12 AMP*

In this instance Daniel mourns for three weeks. This is what we would today consider prayer and fasting except for maybe not quite as dramatic as it appears Daniel did it. God does not respond to pity. His nature is to respond to acts of faith, so whatever we think about how Daniel's mourning was described, he definitely petitioned God for an answer to his prayer and it was definitely done in faith. We know it was because God answered and the angel Gabriel said to Daniel that God had heard him the first day he prayed. Daniel is the perfect example of no matter how short or long we pray, God is looking for the prayer of faith to activate the answer.

As we examine the parable that Jesus uses to teach the disciple about prayer, He interestingly uses a scene that you would see in any government; a courtroom. Typically when you think of going to court you think of a place where an unbiased judge will listen to arguments and render a verdict. I think it's actually funny that Jesus uses an 'unjust' judge in this parable. Could He have used a character that was more opposite of who God is? In fact this man had no respect for God or any man. What does that begin to tell you about this particular type of prayer?

The second character in this parable was a widow woman whose rights had been violated. Now the reason I find this interesting is because as Jesus uncovers this realm of prayer, the object of prayer is not something that this woman wants based on an emotion or a whimsical desire. What she is asking for is something that belongs to her already and she's petitioning the judge to have it returned to her. There is a principle here that we cannot miss! When we petition in prayer for anything, we need to know that it belongs to us before we go to God.

The question a person may ask in this circumstance is, "How do I know what belongs to me?" Here in the United States we have a document called The Constitution. It outlines the rights we have as citizens of this country and when those rights are violated it is the government's job to protect us and restore what belongs to us. Now when we accept Jesus as Lord of our lives, we become citizens of The Kingdom of God and we have a new constitution - **The B-i-b-l-e**.

Now there is a third character in this parable that we can miss if we read too fast and that is what Jesus deems the woman's 'adversary.' An adversary is simply an enemy who is coming against you. In this particular case this adversary came to take away the rights of this widow woman. Just like that widow woman we have an adversary that is satan. He will do everything he can to violate the rights of those who worship God. He used to occupy the position of worshiper before he got puffed up with pride and wanted to receive the worship that only God deserves. However for the record, Luke records Jesus' account of what happened to then Lucifer:

*"And He said to them, "**I saw Satan fall like lightning from heaven**." - Luke 10:18 NKJV*

So to be clear, Satan is powerless as an adversary but he is the underlying force behind the injustice every believer will face at some point during their walk with God. Some of those injustices include sickness, disease, generational curses, addiction, depression, anxiety, and even premature death. None of the things on that list exist in the Kingdom of God because our constitution, the Bible, has laws in it that are completely opposite of these things. So in order to reclaim our rights we have to know the Word of God and be just as persistent as this widow to regain our rights!

*When sickness comes, we have to know that, "...by His stripes **we are healed**." - Isaiah 53:5c NKJV*

*When generational situations happen in your family, we have to know that, "**Christ has redeemed us from the curse of the law**, having become a curse for us..." - Galatians 3:13*

*When depression or anxiety rears its ugly head, we must stand on the law that says, " ...the **peace of God**, which surpasses all understanding, **will guard your hearts and minds through***

Christ Jesus." *Philippians 4:7*

We can go on and on through the Word of God and see who we are and what we have the right to as citizens of the Kingdom. When the adversary comes to steal your health, there is no need to beg God to save you... If you are a citizen of the Kingdom of God sickness is against the law! You just need to know your rights!

The most important part of this prayer comes at the end. I said earlier that every prayer that is offered must be offered in faith. The way Jesus describes it in this passage I totally get why He uses an unjust judge. He wanted to highlight the persistence of the faith of this woman who knew her rights and would not stop petitioning until her rights were restored. The translators named this the parable of the unjust judge, but I think this could just as easily been named the parable of the persistent widow. Her persistent faith in approaching the judge in this parable was so phenomenal that Jesus finished the parable with a staggering question:

"Nevertheless, when the Son of Man comes, **will He really find faith on the earth?"** *- Luke 18:8b NKJV*

The Amplified Bible reads this way:

"However, when the Son of Man comes, ***will He find [this kind of persistent] faith on the earth?"*** *- Luke 18:8b AMP*

Our challenge today is to look at the scripture as more than a religious book. It is to look into the Word of God and keep on looking, until we look into the Word and begin to see a reflection. My prayer is that these very brief and bite sized revelations on prayer will get you on the road to reflection. I pray that as you begin to look more like Jesus, that His image would become obvious to everyone around you. That the world would see Jesus in your eyes, feel Him in your embrace, and hear Him in your voice.

He is a prayer answering God! It is in His nature to answer when you call. Use the very basic principles outlined here to help you in your life of prayer and see your life and the lives of everyone around you begin to change!

"May the LORD bless you and protect you. May the LORD smile on you and be gracious to you. May the LORD show you his favor and give you his peace." - Number 6:24-26 NLT

שָׁלוֹם

5

7 Prayers of Lordship

My Soul, Will, and Emotions

"For those who live according to the flesh **set their minds** on the things of the flesh, but those who live according to the Spirit, the things of the Spirit. For to be carnally minded is death, but **to be spiritually minded is life and peace**." - Romans 8:5-6 NKJV

"**You will keep him in perfect peace**, whose mind stays on You, because he trusts in You." - Isaiah 26:3 NKJV

"**Be anxious for nothing**, but in everything by prayer and supplication, with thanksgiving, let your requests be made known to God; and **the peace of God**, which surpasses all understanding, **will guard your hearts and minds through Christ Jesus**. Finally, brethren, whatever things are true, whatever things are noble, whatever things are just, whatever things are pure, whatever things are lovely, *whatever things are of good report, if there is any virtue and if there is anything praiseworthy—**meditate on these things**." - Philippians 4:6-8 NKJV*

"Lord, I give you complete and total control of my mind, will, and emotions. Holy Spirit I ask you to help me to govern my emotions. Help me to be mindful of my spiritual and mental health and to feed my spirit and soul man with the Word of God. Help me to make following the Word of God a part of my basic instinct and desire. I thank You for peace that I can't even comprehend to guard my heart and my mind. When the enemy comes to try to flood my thoughts I thank you for Your peace that will guard my heart and mind through Christ Jesus. I thank You for keeping me mindful of the wonderful things You have done so that my thoughts stay on You. Let Your Kingdom come and Your will be done in my mind. In Jesus name..."

My Decision making

*"**Trust in the LORD with all your heart**, and lean not on your own understanding; In all your ways acknowledge Him, and **He shall direct your paths**." - Proverbs 3:5-6 NKJV*

*"**If any of you lacks wisdom**, let him ask of God, who gives to all liberally and without reproach, and **it will be given to him**." - James 1:5 NKJV*

*"**The steps of a good man are ordered by the LORD**, and He*

delights in his way. Though he fall, he shall not be utterly cast down; for the LORD upholds him with His hand." - Psalms 37:23-24 NKJV

"Lord, I give You complete and total control of my decision making processes. I know that Your plan for me is perfect and full of hope for the future. So I will not be worried about tomorrow, but I will place tomorrow in Your hands. As I trust You with every decision, I thank You for directing my every step. Holy Spirit I ask for Spiritual wisdom in my decision making, and thank you for a full supply of the wisdom I need for every step I take on the road that You have placed me on. I thank You that every step is ordered by You, so I trust You at all times and in everything! Lord Let Your Kingdom come and Your will be done in every decision I make. In Jesus Name..."

My Finances

*"But this I say: He who sows sparingly will also reap sparingly, and he who sows bountifully will also reap bountifully. So let each one give as he purposes in his heart, not grudgingly or of necessity; for God loves a cheerful giver. And **God is able to make all grace abound toward you, that you, always having all sufficiency in all things, may have an abundance for every good work.**" - 2 Corinthians 9:6-8 NKJV*

*"**Honor the LORD with your possessions**, and with the firstfruits of all your increase; **So your barns will be filled with plenty**, and your vats will overflow with new wine." - Proverbs 3:9-10 NKJV*

"The blessing of the LORD makes one rich, and He adds no sorrow with it." - Proverbs 10:22

*"And all **these blessings shall come upon you and overtake you, because you obey the voice of the LORD your God**: "Blessed shall you be in the city, and blessed shall you be in the country. "Blessed shall be the fruit of your body, the produce of your ground and the increase of your herds, the increase of your cattle and the offspring of your flocks. "Blessed shall be your basket and your kneading bowl. "Blessed shall you be when you come in, and blessed shall you be when you go out." - Deuteronomy 28:2-6*

"Lord, I give You complete and total control of my finances and financial decisions. I know that You supply all of my need and everything I have belongs to You. Lord help me to steward well the supply that I have been entrusted with. It is You that gives me seed to sow and bread to eat. I thank You for a full supply of all of the finances I need to do what You have called me to do. That I would have more than enough for every good work You've called me to. I honor You first with everything I have and for the increase that I experience in my finances. I am blessed because of Your hand on my life and I thank You that blessings continue to overtake me as I obey Your voice. I am unashamedly blessed and I give You all of the glory for continued blessings in my life. Let Your Kingdom come and Your will be done continually in my finances. In Jesus name..."

My Gifts

*"I beseech you therefore, brethren, by the mercies of God, that you **present your bodies a living sacrifice, holy, acceptable to God, which is your reasonable service.** 2 And do not be conformed to this world, but be transformed by the renewing of your mind, that you may prove what is that good and acceptable and perfect will of God." - Romans 12:1-2 NKJV*

*"**As each one has received a gift, minister it to one another, as good stewards of the manifold grace of God.** If anyone speaks, let him speak as the oracles of God. If anyone ministers, **let him do it as with the ability which God supplies, that in all things God may be glorified through Jesus Christ**, to whom belong the glory and the dominion forever and ever. Amen." - 1 Peter 4:10-11*

*"For as we have many members in one body, but **all the members do not have the same function**, so we, being many, are one body in Christ, and individually members of one another. **Having then gifts differing according to the grace that is given to us, let us use them...**" - Romans 12:4-6a*

"Lord, I give You complete and total control of the gifts that You have placed in me. I take this gift that You have placed inside of me and I give it back to You. I commit to use this gift to serve those You have called me to serve. I thank You for opening doors of opportunity to display Your love for others through me. I thank You for Your anointing on my life to display this gift unashamedly and bring glory to You in the process. Holy Spirit help me to complete and not compete with

the gift you have entrusted me with so that the You will be seen in everything I do. Let Your Kingdom come and Your will be done through this gift and calling on my life. In Jesus name..."

My Body

"Or do you not know that **your body is the temple of the Holy Spirit** who is in you, whom you have from God, and you are not your own? For you were bought at a price; therefore **glorify God in your body** and in your spirit, which are God's." - 1 Corinthians 6:19-20 NKJV

"**I discipline my body and bring it into subjection**, lest, when I have preached to others, I myself should become disqualified." - 1 Corinthians 9:27 NKJV

"Now no discipline seems to be joyful for the present, but painful; nevertheless, afterward **it yields the peaceable fruit of righteousness** to those who have been trained by it." - Hebrews 12:11 NKJV

"Lord, I give You complete and total control of my body and all of its desires. I come boldly now to the throne of grace especially in time when my flesh is weak. I am your temple Holy Spirit, so I give You permission to turn over the tables of my heart and deal with my weakness. Help me to glorify You in my body. Help me to see the areas where I need to be more disciplined in my habits and empower me to be stronger in my Spirit and Soul everyday to maintain that discipline. I thank You for continuing to strengthen my body and giving me

wisdom to rest when needed. Let Your Kingdom come and Your will be done in my body. In Jesus name..."

My priorities

*"Therefore do not worry, saying, 'What shall we eat?' or 'What shall we drink?' or 'What shall we wear?' For after all these things the Gentiles seek. For your heavenly Father knows that you need all these things. But **seek first the kingdom of God and His righteousness**, and all these things shall be added to you." - Matthew 6:-31-33 NKJV*

*"**I am the LORD your God, who brought you out** of the land of Egypt, out of the house of bondage. "**You shall have no other gods before Me.**" - Exodus 20:2-3*

*"And **do not be conformed to this world, but be transformed by the renewing of your mind**, that you may prove what is that good and acceptable and perfect will of God." - Romans 12:2*

*"Now it happened as they went that He entered a certain village; and a certain woman named Martha welcomed Him into her house. And she had a sister called Mary, **who also sat at Jesus' feet and heard His word.** But Martha was distracted with much serving, and she approached Him and said, "Lord, do You not care that my sister has left me to serve alone? Therefore tell her to help me." And Jesus answered and said to her, "Martha, Martha, **you are worried and troubled about many things. But one thing is needed**, and Mary has chosen that good part, which will not be taken away from*

her." Luke 10:38-42

"Lord, I give You complete and total control of my priorities. I commit to put my list in You. I ask You to be in everything that I do, in every area of my life. Holy Spirit help me to identify and discern opportunities that are right for me and the plan that You have for my life. Lord my desire is always to be in right standing with You, so rule and reign as King in my heart. Thank you for bringing me out of darkness into the light, out of fear into Your love for me, and out of bondage into freedom! Help me to see Your hand in everything I do and to never step outside the boundaries set in Your Word to 'make it happen.' I give You my heart and every desire to use for Your glory. Let Your Kingdom come and Your will be done in my priorities. In Jesus name..."

My Relationships

"Love suffers long and is kind; love does not envy; love does not parade itself, is not puffed up; does not behave rudely, does not seek its own, is not provoked, thinks no evil; does not rejoice in iniquity, but rejoices in the truth; bears all things, believes all things, hopes all things, endures all things. **Love never fails.**" - 1 Corinthians 13:4-8a NKJV

"The discretion of a man makes him slow to anger, and **his glory is to overlook a transgression.**" - Proverbs 19:11 NKJV

"*Two are better than one, because they have a good reward for* *their labor. For if they fall, **one will lift up his companion**, but woe to him who is alone when he falls, for he has no one to help him up. Again, if two lie down together, they will keep warm; but how can one be warm alone? Though one may be overpowered by another, two can withstand him. **And a threefold cord is not quickly broken.***" - *Ecclesiastes 4:9-12 NKJV*

*"These things I have spoken to you, **that My joy may remain in you**, and that your joy may be full. This is My commandment, that you **love one another as I have loved you**. Greater love has no one than this, than to **lay down one's life for his friends**." John 15:11-13 NKJV*

"Lord, I give You complete and total control of my relationships. As I continue to seek first Your Kingdom I thank you for relationships that will cause me to maintain my focus on you. I thank You for relationships ordained by You. I thank You for the people that You have placed in my life to mentor and teach me to be more Christ-like in every area of my life. I thank You for friends that sharpen me, like iron sharpens iron and friends that are just as focused on You as I am. Lord, I also thank you for those that You have put in my path for me to mentor or even just introduce to You. Lord, give me wisdom in every relationship to continue to keep my eyes on You, and give me the strength to eliminate relationships that are not good for me in this season. Holy Spirit help me to walk in love and remain unoffendable when there is miscommunication. Help me to see the best in others and protect me from the pretense in those that would come to try to throw me off course. Help me to draw close to You and maintain joy in tough situations with others. Be glorified in my thoughts toward every person I am

in relationship with. Let Your Kingdom come and Your will be done in my relationships. In Jesus name..."

6

7 Prayers of Intercession

My Family and Friends

"*Again, departing from the region of Tyre and Sidon, He came through the midst of the region of Decapolis to the Sea of Galilee.* **Then they brought to Him** *one who was deaf and had an impediment in his speech, and* **they begged Him to put His hand on him.**" *- Mark 7:31-32 NKJV*

"*Let Your work appear to Your servants, and* **Your glory to their children.** *And let the beauty of the* **LORD our God be upon us, and establish the work of our hands for us**; *yes, establish the work of our hands.*" *- Psalms 90:16-17 NKJV*

"*No weapon formed against you shall prosper, and every tongue which rises against you in judgment you shall condemn.* **This is the heritage of the servants of the LORD, and their righteousness is from Me,**" *says the LORD.*" *- Isaiah 54:17 NKJV*

"Therefore, as the elect of God, holy and beloved, **put on tender mercies, kindness, humility, meekness, longsuffering; bearing with one another, and forgiving one another,** *if anyone has a complaint against another; even as Christ forgave you, so you also must do. But above all these things* **put on love, which is the bond of perfection. And let the peace of God rule in your hearts**, *to which also you were called in one body; and* **be thankful."** *- Colossians 3:12-15 NKJV*

"Lord, I come to You on behalf of my family and friends. I ask that You would continue to reveal Yourself to them so that they may recognize You as the only true and living God. Lord they have need of things that I know of and things that I don't, but You are the one who supplies every need according to Your riches in glory by Christ Jesus. So I ask for a full supply be granted to them and that they recognize that it is You who have established the work of their hands. I rebuke every assignment that the enemy has set against them and I thank You that you have given Your angels charge over them. I thank You that no weapon formed against them will have any effect on the path You have put them on. Lord let Your peace rule in their hearts, minds, and households. I stand in the gap for Your will to be established in them. In Jesus name..."

My Neighbors and Co-workers

"We then who are strong ought to bear with the scruples of the weak, and not to please ourselves. **Let each of us please his neighbor for his good, leading to edification."** *- Romans 15:1-2 NKJV*

*"So he answered and said, " 'You shall love the LORD your God with all your heart, with all your soul, with all your strength, and with all your mind,' **and 'your neighbor as yourself.'** " - Luke 10:27 NKJV*

*"Therefore if there is any consolation in Christ, if any comfort of love, if any fellowship of the Spirit, if any affection and mercy, **fulfill my joy by being like-minded, having the same love, being of one accord, of one mind**. Let nothing be done through selfish ambition or conceit, but in lowliness of mind **let each esteem others better than himself**. Let each of you look out not only for his own interests, but also **for the interests of others**." - Philippians 2:1-4 NKJV*

*"As you therefore have received Christ Jesus the Lord, **so walk in Him, rooted and built up in Him and established in the faith**, as you have been taught, abounding in it with thanksgiving." - Colossian 2:6-7 NKJV*

"Lord, I come to You on behalf of my neighbors and co-workers. Lord, I pray that You would surround them with people that would point them to You. Jesus because You were lifted on the cross for them You said You would draw them unto Yourself. I thank You for that continued drawing and that You would even put words in my mouth that You desire for them to hear. Let Your love shine bright in my life and the lives of others around them, that they would receive You as King in their own lives. I thank You also for those that have a relationship with You already, that their joy would be full. I thank you for Your favor on their lives and that they would be rooted and established in You! I stand in the gap for Your will to be continually established in them. In Jesus name..."

My Church and my Pastor

"Now I am no longer in the world, but these are in the world, and I come to You. Holy Father, keep through Your name those whom You have given Me, **that they may be one as We are.**" - John 17:11 NKJV

"Assuredly, I say to you, whatever you bind on earth will be bound in heaven, and whatever you loose on earth will be loosed in heaven. "Again I say to you that **if two of you agree on earth concerning anything that they ask, it will be done for them by My Father in heaven.** For where two or three are gathered together in My name, **I am there in the midst of them.**" - Matthew 18:18-20 NKJV

"**Obey those who rule over you,** and be submissive, **for they watch out for your souls,** as those who must give account. **Let them do so with joy** and not with grief, for that would be unprofitable for you." - Hebrews 13:17 NKJV

"**Let the elders who rule well be counted worthy of double honor, especially those who labor in the word and doctrine.** For the Scripture says, "You shall not muzzle an ox while it treads out the grain," and, "The laborer is worthy of his wages." - 1 Timothy 5:17-18 NKJV

"Lord, I come to You on behalf of my church and my Pastor. I pray first for unity in our church, that we would be united by Your Spirit and walk in agreement. Your word says that a house divided against itself will not stand. So I rebuke any sort of discord that would bring division in our body of

believers. Help us to see clearly the need for each other as we continue to point the world to the wonderful things You have done for us. Jesus You prayed that we would be one so that the world would be able to see You for who you really are. So I ask that You would guide our leadership with Your wisdom in moving forward into what You have called us to do as a church. I pray for my Pastor that You would surround him and his family with a hedge of protection. Lord I ask that every need spoken or unspoken would be fully supplied and that You continue to strengthen them for the function that You have called them to in this season. Surround them with strong and wise leadership who hear from You and provide sound counsel to my Pastor when needed. I stand in the gap for Your will to continually be established in them. In Jesus name..."

The Lost

*"The Lord is not slack concerning His promise, as some count slackness, but is longsuffering toward us, **not willing that any should perish but that all should come to repentance.**" 2 Peter 3:9 NKJV*

*"What man of you, having a hundred sheep, if he loses one of them, does not **leave the ninety-nine in the wilderness, and go after the one which is lost until he finds it?** And when he has found it, he lays it on his shoulders, rejoicing. And when he comes home, he calls together his friends and neighbors, saying to them, 'Rejoice with me, for I have found my sheep which was lost!' I say to you that likewise **there will be more joy in heaven over one sinner who***

repents *than over ninety-nine just persons who need no repentance."*
- Luke 15:4-7 NKJV

"But God demonstrates His own love toward us, in that **while we were still sinners, Christ died for us**." - Romans 5:8 NKJV

"And Jesus said to him, "Today salvation has come to this house, because he also is a son of Abraham; for **the Son of Man has come to seek and to save that which was lost**." - Luke 19:9-10 NKJV

"Lord, I come to You on behalf of the lost in my community. Lord, Your commission to us is to go into the world and preach the gospel and make disciples. So I pray for continued open doors of opportunity to speak into the lives of those who do not know You. Holy Spirit I ask for Your help to be a witness for the Kingdom to every person You put in my path. Jesus You said that You would leave the 99 to find the one. I commit today to being a part of your search party. I pray that as the gospel of the Kingdom is presented, ready hearts will turn in faith and receive you as King in their lives! I stand in the gap for Your will to continually be established in them. In Jesus name..."

Our Government

"Therefore I exhort first of all that supplications, prayers, intercessions, and giving of thanks be made for all men, **for kings and all who are in authority**, that we may lead a quiet and peaceable life in all godliness and reverence." - 1 Timothy 2:1-2 NKJV

*"**Righteousness exalts a nation**, but sin is a reproach to any people."*
- Proverbs 14:34 NKJV

*"For unto us a Child is born, Unto us a Son is given; and **the government will be upon His shoulder.** And His name will be called Wonderful, Counselor, Mighty God, Everlasting Father, Prince of Peace. **Of the increase of His government and peace there will be no end,** upon the throne of David and over His kingdom, to order it and establish it with judgment and justice from that time forward, even forever. The zeal of the LORD of hosts will perform this." - Isaiah 9:6-7 NKJV*

*"**The king's heart is in the hand of the LORD**, like the rivers of water; He turns it wherever He wishes." - Proverbs 21:1 NKJV*

"Lord, I come to You on behalf of our city, state and national governments. Your word says that intercession should be made for all who are in authority. So Lord I ask that you would protect our leaders from harm and reveal Yourself to them in a special way. I ask You to grant them supernatural wisdom to govern with Your authority. Lord I ask that You would install righteous leaders who would be men and women after Your heart. I also ask that You would surround these leaders with men and women who walk in Spiritual wisdom and relationship with You. Lord, I ask that You would uproot every kind of corruption and expose every agenda operating in darkness. I pray for righteous leaders to return to every level and branch of government including our legislative, judicial and executive branches. I place the heart of our leaders in Your hand and pray for peace, unity, and mass repentance from sin in our government. I stand in the gap for

Your will to be continually established in every part of our government. In Jesus name..."

Our Military

*"Only **be strong and very courageous**, that you may observe to do according to all the law which Moses My servant commanded you; do not turn from it to the right hand or to the left, that you may prosper wherever you go. This Book of the Law shall not depart from your mouth, but **you shall meditate in it day and night, that you may observe to do according to all that is written in it. For then you will make your way prosperous, and then you will have good success**. Have I not commanded you? Be strong and of good courage; do not be afraid, nor be dismayed, for **the LORD your God is with you wherever you go**." - Joshua 1:7-9 NKJV*

*"LORD, how they have increased who trouble me! Many are they who rise up against me. Many are they who say of me, "There is no help for him in God." Selah. But **You, O LORD, are a shield for me, My glory and the One who lifts up my head. I cried to the LORD with my voice, and He heard me from His holy hill**." Psalms 3:1-4 NKJV*

*"Whenever I am afraid, **I will trust in You**. In God (I will praise His word), In God I have put my trust; **I will not fear**. What can flesh do to me?" - Psalms 56:3-4 NKJV*

"Lord, I come to You on behalf of our Military service men and women. I pray Your hand of protection would be on them as

they defend our nation. I ask that You would reveal Yourself to each one so that they would know a relationship with You means that they are never alone. Help them to be strong and courageous both in battle and out. Protect their minds from long term trauma and mental breakdown as they put their trust in You. Keep them free from immoral influences and keep them physically healthy and free from sickness and disease. Speak to them in the field and give them supernatural wisdom so they can see and hear clearly to carry out their mission. I stand in the gap for Your will to continually be established in our military. In Jesus name..."

The Whole Church

"*...that the God of our Lord Jesus Christ, the Father of glory, **may give to you the spirit of wisdom and revelation in the knowledge of Him, the eyes of your understanding being enlightened; that you may know what is the hope of His calling, what are the riches of the glory of His inheritance in the saints, and what is the exceeding greatness of His power toward us who believe**, according to the working of His mighty power..." - Ephesians 1:17-19 NKJV*

"*And this I pray, **that your love may abound still more and more in knowledge and all discernment, that you may approve the things that are excellent, that you may be sincere and without offense till the day of Christ**, being filled with the fruits of righteousness which are by Jesus Christ, to the glory and praise of God." - Philippians 1:9-11 NKJV*

*"For this reason we also, since the day we heard it, do not cease to pray for you, and to ask **that you may be filled with the knowledge of His will in all wisdom and spiritual understanding; that you may walk worthy of the Lord, fully pleasing Him, being fruitful in every good work and increasing in the knowledge of God; strengthened with all might, according to His glorious power, for all patience and longsuffering with joy;** giving thanks to the Father who has qualified us to be partakers of the inheritance of the saints in the light." - Colossian 1:9-12 NKJV*

"Lord, I come to You on behalf of the whole church, Your bride, the body of Christ. I pray according to Your word that we would become one, just as You and the Father are one so that the world would know that You came for them. As you reveal Yourself everyday to us, I thank You for the empowerment by the Holy Spirit to be a witness to the world. Holy Spirit I pray that You would help us through the Word and by Your Spirit to prepare our hearts to labor in this time of incredible harvest. Help us to be wise with the things we give our time to. Help us to live accurately according to Your word and stir up a hunger in our hearts for more of You. Help us to produce the fruit of righteousness that truly differentiates us from the world, that Your love would overflow from Your Church. Help us to walk worthy of the calling that You have for each of us individually so that we are complete and mature, displaying Your glory for all the world to see. Help Your church to shine brighter than ever before that we might show up like Jesus everywhere we go. I stand in the gap for Your will to continually be established in Your church. In Jesus name..."

7

7 Prayers of Petition

Health and Healing

"...who Himself bore our sins in His own body on the tree, that we, having died to sins, might live for righteousness—**by whose stripes you were healed.**" - 1 Peter 2:24 NKJV

"Surely He has borne our griefs and carried our sorrows; yet we esteemed Him stricken, smitten by God, and afflicted. But **He was wounded for our transgressions, He was bruised for our iniquities; the chastisement for our peace was upon Him**, and by His stripes we are healed." - Isaiah 53:4-5 NKJV

For **I will restore health to you and heal you** of your wounds,' says the LORD," - Jeremiah 30:17 NKJV

"And if Christ is in you, the body is dead because of sin, but the Spirit is life because of righteousness. But if the Spirit of Him who raised

Jesus from the dead dwells in you, **He who raised Christ from the dead will also give life to your mortal bodies through His Spirit who dwells in you.**" - Romans 8:10-11 NKJV

"Then they cried out to the LORD in their trouble, and He saved them out of their distresses. **He sent His word and healed them, and delivered them from their destructions.** Oh, that men would give thanks to the LORD for His goodness, and for His wonderful works to the children of men!" - Psalms 107:19-21 NKJV

"Lord, I enter Your court with praise because You alone are worthy of all of the praise. I have come also because an adversary has broken the law of Your Word and attempted to steal my health and healing. According to Your Word in Isaiah 53:4, I am healed by Your stripes, and according to Romans 8:11, You give life to my mortal body through Your Spirit that dwells in me. For that reason I stand in this court with my Advocate who has paid the price for my healing and petition the court for my health to be restored and to line up with Your Word. I praise You in advance because I know that You are a righteous judge and Your Word is true! In Jesus name..."

Protection

"He who dwells in the secret place of the Most High shall abide under the shadow of the Almighty. I will say of the LORD, "**He is my refuge and my fortress; My God, in Him I will trust.**" **Surely He shall deliver you from the snare of the fowler and from the perilous pestilence.** He shall cover you with His feathers, and under

His wings you shall take refuge; His truth shall be your shield and buckler." - Psalms 91:1-4 NKJV

*"**No weapon formed against you shall prosper, and every tongue which rises against you in judgment you shall condemn.** This is the heritage of the servants of the LORD, and their righteousness is from Me," Says the LORD." - Isaiah 54:17 NKJV*

*"Finally, brethren, pray for us, that the word of the Lord may run swiftly and be glorified, just as it is with you, and that we may be delivered from unreasonable and wicked men; for not all have faith. **But the Lord is faithful, who will establish you and guard you from the evil one.**" - 2 Thessalonians 3:3 NKJV*

*"And Moses said to the people, "**Do not be afraid. Stand still, and see the salvation of the LORD**, which He will accomplish for you today. For the Egyptians whom you see today, you shall see again no more forever. **The LORD will fight for you, and you shall hold your peace.**" - Exodus 14:13-14 NKJV*

> *"Lord, I enter Your court with praise because You alone are worthy of all of the praise. I have come also because an adversary has broken the law of Your Word and attempted to steal my promise of protection. According to Your Word in Psalms 91:11, You have given angels charge over me and in 2 Thessalonians 3:3, You will establish and guard me from the evil one. For that reason I stand in this court with my Advocate who has paid the price for my protection and petition the court for my protection to be restored and to line up with Your Word. I praise You in advance because I know that You are a righteous judge and Your Word is true! In Jesus name..."*

Financial Provision

*"And **my God shall supply all your need** according to His riches in glory by Christ Jesus." - Philippians 4:19 NKJV*

*"And God is able to make all grace abound toward you, that you, always having all sufficiency in all things, **may have an abundance for every good work**." - 2 Corinthians 9:8 NKJV*

*"**But seek first the kingdom of God and His righteousness, and all these things shall be added to you.** Therefore do not worry about tomorrow, for tomorrow will worry about its own things. Sufficient for the day is its own trouble." - Matthew 6:33-34 NKJV*

*"Oh, taste and see that **the LORD is good**; Blessed is the man who trusts in Him! Oh, fear the LORD, you His saints! **There is no want to those who fear Him**. The young lions lack and suffer hunger; But **those who seek the LORD shall not lack any good thing**." - Psalms 34:8-10*

"Lord, I enter Your court with praise because You alone are worthy of all of the praise. I have come also because an adversary has broken the law of Your Word and attempted to steal my promise financial provision. According to Your Word in Philippians 4:19, You God are the one Who supplies all of my need according to Your riches in glory by Christ Jesus and Matthew 6:33 says that if I seek first Your Kingdom and righteousness then all I need will be supplied. For that reason I stand in this court with my Advocate who has paid the price for my financial provision and petition the court for my

financial provision to be restored and to line up with Your Word. I praise You in advance because I know that You are a righteous judge and Your Word is true! In Jesus name..."

Peace

*"**You will keep him in perfect peace, whose mind is stayed on You**, because he trusts in You. Trust in the LORD forever, For in YAH, the LORD, is everlasting strength." - Isaiah 26:3-4 NKJV*

*"**Peace I leave with you, My peace I give to you**; not as the world gives do I give to you. Let not your heart be troubled, neither let it be afraid." - John 14:27 NKJV*

*"For to be carnally minded is death, but **to be spiritually minded is life and peace.**" - Romans 8:6 NKJV*

*"The LORD will give strength to His people; **the LORD will bless His people with peace.**" - Psalms 29:11 NKJV*

*"Be anxious for nothing, but in everything by prayer and supplication, with thanksgiving, let your requests be made known to God; **and the peace of God, which surpasses all understanding, will guard your hearts and minds through Christ Jesus.**" - Philippians 4:6-7 NKJV*

"Lord, I enter Your court with praise because You alone are worthy of all of the praise. I have come also because an adversary has broken the law of Your Word and attempted to

steal my promise of peace. According to Your Word in Isaiah 26:3 as long as I keep my mind stayed on You, You will keep me in perfect peace and Philippians 4:6-7 says that as long as I come to You in prayer making my request known to You, that Your peace will guard my heart and mind through Christ Jesus. For that reason I stand in this court with my Advocate who has paid the price for my peace and petition the court for my peace to be restored and to line up with Your Word. I praise You in advance because I know that You are a righteous judge and Your Word is true! In Jesus name..."

Long Life

"Because he has set his love upon Me, therefore I will deliver him; I will set him on high, because he has known My name. He shall call upon Me, and I will answer him; I will be with him in trouble; I will deliver him and honor him. **With long life I will satisfy him, and show him My salvation."** *- Psalms 91 91:14-16 NKJV*

"You shall walk in all the ways which the LORD your God has commanded you, *that you may live and that it may be well with you, and* **that you may prolong your days in the land which you shall possess."** *- Deuteronomy 5:33 NKJV*

"So you shall serve the LORD your God, and He will bless your bread and your water. And I will take sickness away from the midst of you. No one shall suffer miscarriage or be barren in your land; **I will fulfill the number of your days."** *- Exodus 23:25-26 NKJV*

"The thief does not come except to steal, and to kill, and to destroy. **I have come that they may have life, and that they may have it more abundantly.***"* *- John 10:10 NKJV*

"Now this is the commandment, and these are the statutes and judgments which the LORD your God has commanded to teach you, that you may observe them in the land which you are crossing over to possess, that you may fear the LORD your God, to keep all His statutes and His commandments which I command you, you and your son and your grandson, all the days of your life, and **that your days may be prolonged.***"* *- Deuteronomy 6:1-2 NKJV*

"For You meet him with the blessings of goodness; You set a crown of pure gold upon his head. **He asked life from You, and You gave it to him—length of days forever and ever.***"* *- Psalms 21:3-4 NKJV*

> ***"Lord, I enter Your court with praise because You alone are worthy of all of the praise. I have come also because an adversary has broken the law of Your Word and attempted to steal my promise of long life. According to Your Word in Psalm 91:16, You said if I call You will answer and with long life You will satisfy me and You said of the King in Psalms 21:3-4, He asked for long life and You gave it to him. For that reason I stand in this court with my Advocate who has paid the price for my long life and petition the court for my long life to be restored and my health to line up with Your Word. I praise You in advance because I know that You are a righteous judge and Your Word is true! In Jesus name..."***

Joy

"You will show me the path of life; **in Your presence is fullness of joy;** *at Your right hand are pleasures forevermore." - Psalms 16:11 NKJV*

*"****But the fruit of the Spirit*** *is love,* ***joy****, peace, longsuffering, kindness, goodness, faithfulness, gentleness, self-control.* ***Against such there is no law.****" - Galatians 5:22-23 NKJV*

"Therefore do not let your good be spoken of as evil; for ***the kingdom of God is*** *not eating and drinking, but righteousness and peace and* ***joy in the Holy Spirit.****" - Romans 14:16-17 NKJV*

*"****In this you greatly rejoice, though now for a little while, if need be, you have been grieved by various trials, that the genuineness of your faith, being much more precious than gold that perishes, though it is tested by fire, may be found to praise, honor, and glory at the revelation of Jesus Christ, whom having not seen you love.*** *Though now you do not see Him, yet believing,* ***you rejoice with joy inexpressible and full of glory****, receiving the end of your faith—the salvation of your souls." - 1 Peter 1:6-9 NKJV*

"My brethren, ***count it all joy*** *when you fall into various trials..." - James 1:2 NKJV*

> *"Lord, I enter Your court with praise because You alone are worthy of all of the praise. I have come also because an adversary has broken the law of Your Word and attempted to steal my joy. According to Your Word in Psalms 16:11 as long*

as I'm in Your presence I will be full of Joy and Galatians 5:22 tell me that Joy is a fruit growing because of Your Spirit presiding over my life. For that reason I stand in this court with my Advocate who has paid the price for my joy and petition the court for my joy to be restored. I praise You in advance because I know that You are a righteous judge and Your Word is true! In Jesus name..."

Rest

"Come to Me, all you who labor and are heavy laden, and **I will give you rest**. Take My yoke upon you and learn from Me, for I am gentle and lowly in heart, and **you will find rest for your souls**. For My yoke is easy and My burden is light." - Matthew 11:28-30 NKJV

"**Unless the LORD builds the house, they labor in vain who build it**; unless the LORD guards the city, The watchman stays awake in vain. It is vain for you to rise up early, to sit up late,

To eat the bread of sorrows; **for so He gives His beloved sleep**." - Psalms 127:1-2 NKJV

"**There remains therefore a rest for the people of God.** For he who has entered His rest has himself also ceased from his works as God did from His. Let us therefore **be diligent to enter that rest**, lest anyone fall according to the same example of disobedience." - Hebrews 4:9-11 NKJV

For thus says the Lord GOD, the Holy One of Israel: **"In returning and rest you shall be saved; in quietness and confidence shall be your strength."** *- Isaiah 30:15 NKJV*

"Lord, I enter Your court with praise because You alone are worthy of all of the praise. I have come also because an adversary has broken the law of Your Word and attempted to steal my joy. According to Your Word in Matthew 11:28-30, You will give me rest when I come to You and learn from You, and in Psalm 127:2, You said that you give Your beloved peace. For that reason I stand in this court with my Advocate who has paid the price for my rest and petition the court for my rest to be restored. I praise You in advance because I know that You are a righteous judge and Your Word is true! In Jesus name..."

8

Conclusion

My prayer for you is that whether you are a seasoned citizen of the Kingdom or are new to your faith in Jesus, you have received some revelation or exhortation that will propel you forward in a life of prayer. These 21 prayers that I finished with, should be just the start for you. If you haven't already… let this book be your call to action and live a life of prayer because, **PRAYER WORKS**!

If this book has blessed you please be sure to pass it on to someone else that may benefit from its contents and be sure to leave me a positive Amazon review to let me know your feedback.

May the King Bless your life!

Pastor Alex

Made in the USA
Middletown, DE
12 March 2025